Micro Wind Turbine:

A Beginner's Guide to Build a Micro Wind Turbine

Table of Contents

Introduction: Micro Wind Turbines in Brief

Everyone has to start somewhere, so where then, does a potential wind enthusiast start? Well, you can start with your own backyard, because the first thing you should take stock of when you are considering the construction of your own micro wind turbine should be the actual amount of land space that you have to work with. You have to have at least a small, flat portion of land in order for any micro wind turbine project to be successful.

After that consideration has been made, you should probably consider who in your nearby vicinity a wind turbine might affect; namely your neighbors. With the neighbors consulted you should check up on the local zoning and building regulations of your community (Which will be discussed more in depth later in this book).

Once these prerequisite check boxes have been checked however, you are as good as gold. Get your parts from the local hardware store and your own garage, and build your micro wind turbine! This is the briefest summary you will ever get when it comes to what makes a successful micro wind turbine project. This is the skeleton on which the meat of your project will be hung. Now buy this book to find out the rest!

Chapter 1: Understanding and Preparing for Wind Energy

As we hear it rustling through the branches, most of us think that we know what wind is, but besides the more rudimentary reaction of our senses, when we get down to it, most of us don't really know what wind is. The wind is actually a byproduct of the sun's rays moving through our planet's atmosphere. When charged particles from the sun hit different pockets of atmospheric pressure in the Earth's atmosphere, wind is created. In this chapter we are going to further explore some of the finer aspects of how wind is used to make energy.

The Wind Force Scale

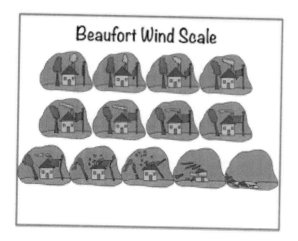

It was a man named Francis Beaufort who created the first known wind force scale, in which he rated the wind on a scale from 0 to 12, with 0 indicating virtually no wind at all and 12 designating maximum hurricane force winds.

This scale was subsequently expanded later on to 17 levels but the original 0 to 12 is more than sufficient when it comes to rating the winds that your turbine might encounter.

For the most part, the best place for any wind turbine to be in on this scale would be right around 5 or 6, which would constitute a fairly robust, breezy wind. Frequent winds at 7 and above may provide you with some great energy after a while, but such high winds over long periods of time could also potentially damage your wind turbine, causing structural damage such as bent or broken rotor blades. So I the case of wind, it is always best to shoot for the happy medium, right in the middle of the wind force scale.

How Wind Turbines Work

The wind turbine is one of the best ways to capture wind energy. It is amazingly simple and yet surprisingly efficient. And at the most basic level the function of a wind turbine can be summed up like this; wind blows, this blowing wind causes the rotor blades of the turbine to spin, when these blades spin, they in turn cause a shaft inside the device to turn, the kinetic motion of which causes energy to be transferred directly to a generator which coverts that energy into electricity.

If you think about it, this whole process is actually working as an electric house fan in reverse. Yes, it could be said that the common electric house fan that you might plug in during the summer to cool off, works in the complete opposite order of how a wind turbine functions. And it also creates the exact opposite result.

Just think about it. You plug a house fan into your electric outlet in the wall, the electric current then causes the blades of the fan to spin, and this spinning creates the wind that you desire in order to cool yourself off! This is the complete opposite of how a wind turbine works! An electric fan uses electricity to create wind, but a wind turbine uses wind to create electricity!

How Wind Energy Can Help your Bottom Line

Of course, we only do things if they benefit our lives, this is a given, so having that said, just how much can wind energy benefit us? Well, the simple answer to this is; it depends.

Depending on the size of your tower, the amount of turbines, and the wind speed on your area, the net amount of energy you accumulate will ultimately vary.

But with optimal wind conditions and at least one viable wind turbine there is no reason you can't routinely produce at least 50 kilowatts of power. This is more than enough energy for the average household for an entire year. But if you would still like to know exactly how much energy you might be able to generate, you are going to have to crunch some numbers.

Because there is a special equation that has been created for just such a task, simply multiple energy efficiently by wind speed, density of air, and how long your blades are, and you will soon get a better idea of how wind energy can help your bottom line. Just crunch the numbers and punch in this simple equation if you have any questions about what wind energy can do for you!

Environmental and Energy Considerations

Since wind turbines are only using something that already exists naturally anyway; wind and air turbulence, there is no contamination or pollution as a byproduct.

Wind power has no waste, and nothing extra is introduced into the environment in order to create it, making for the cleanest energy source you could ever come by.

The industrialized world is slowly coming to the conclusion that the past 200 years of Fossil Fuel use is going to soon come to an end. But that's ok, because the renewable energy of wind power is waiting right there to take its place. Unlike the mountain depleting coal mines of North America, wind does not subtract from the environmental landscape.

As much as wind is utilized, this natural and renewable part of Earth's biosphere will keep right on blowing back in our faces time and time again. Wind energy can save the environment and save our money all at the same time! These are great and exciting things to consider when you prepare to make the most of your wind energy.

Making Your Residence More Energy Efficient

Making your home more energy efficient should go hand in hand with producing wind energy. Really it's just common sense; the more efficient your home is in using energy the better it can benefit from the energy that you produce.

So in order to maximize your returns from your wind turbine, let's take a look at making that home of yours as energy efficient as it can be.

And in doing this, one of the first things you should take into consideration is your home's insulation. The winter months can have us paying a lot on our heat and electric bills, but if we would just make sure that our home is properly insulated in the first place, much of this expenditure can be eliminated.

So it would be wise to take inventory of just what kind of insulation you have, and probe your home's entire structure for any weak spots where the insulation is lacking or thinning.

Make sure your home is retaining heat, so you don't waste your energy. Along with heat, you should also take a look at how much energy you are using when it comes to keeping your house lit. Believe it or not, something as simple as changing your light bulbs could in fact save you a whole lot of money.

Fluorescent light bulbs have been proven to make a big difference, and can significantly reduce the wattage that is used.

These bulbs can be found at most department and hardware stores. It wouldn't hurt to stock up on a few of them. It also wouldn't hurt to take a realistic inventory of how energy efficient your home appliances are.

One good key in this is to try and make sure that you have appliances that are officially labeled as "Energy Star" efficient. This classification means that the EPA (Environmental Protection Agency) has officially sanctioned its use, noting the efficiency of the product.

Checking for Energy Star designations can then be followed up by assessing the rest of your home electronics, taking note of what devices might be using up the most energy. All of these measures will help you to make your home more energy efficient. Be diligent in using them so that you will have a good template on which to begin your micro wind turbine project.

Chapter 2: Constructing Your Micro Wind Turbine

With all of the preliminary information digested, you can now move on to the main course, and learn how to construct your very own micro wind turbine. It doesn't take much material, but it does take some patience and a fine attention to detail, so please pay attention to what you'll find in this chapter!

Rotor Blades

The blades are the conductors of your energy, so you have to be able to get them right, creating the precise shape and design that will facility this transfer of power.

These blades when constructed properly should be able to transform about half of all motion into electric power. But in order to be efficient your rotor blades have to be able to move rapidly through the air uninhibited.

The best way to achieve this rapid, uninhibited motion is to make sure that your micro wind turbine is evenly balanced. This can be most easily achieved through the use of "tip speed ratio" or as it is abbreviated "TSR".

Using a TSR allows you to align the motion of your blades with the speed of the wind. With this knowledge you can then customize your blades to where if you have a blade that is 7 feet long, you can use this ration to better match these measurements.

With tip ratio's established you can then work on shaping your blades, tapering the rotor blade from its tip all the way down to its very base. Most blades are either composed of wood or PVC pipe. The only problem with wood is that sometimes it can crack and develop other aberrations on its surface, so if wood is your first choice, just be sure to check the material for any defects before use.

In order to avoid these problems altogether however, you could opt for PVC pipe. This material is easy to obtain at any hardware store and is the same exact kid of piping found in the plumbing of your home. Just take a piece of PVC pipe and a utensil to carve it with and begin fleshing out your blade from the pointed tip to the wider mid section and then on down to the more narrow base. This narrow base will work to stabilize the entire structure of the blade.

Fixing the Blades to Their Rotor

With each blade fleshed out you can then move on to affixing them to their rotor. The rotor itself should be a triangle so that your blades can attach in at 95 degree descending angles.

Once this has been established you should then drill some holes in the center of the rotor. This is where your blades will be attached to the rotor. Make sure that these blades are firmly attached; the last thing you want is your blade to suddenly fly off and hit your neighbor's house! (Or even worse than that; your neighbor!) So please be careful, and make sure that these blades are firmly attached to their rotor.

Setting Up your Wind Turbine's Tower

The tower for your wind turbine can have a direct impact on your level of production. The higher your turbine can be placed on a tower, the more effective the wind energy from that turbine can be. But having that said, you really don't want to place your blades too high because this will ultimately lead to undesired turbulence and possible damage to your blades.

As a rule, you generally want your turbine to be placed just high enough to take advantage of higher winds, but yet still low enough to avoid excessive gusts. Typically a height of 10 feet should be enough to fulfill both of these requirements.

The best middle ground in this however, would be to invest in a tilt tower. A tilt tower is a tower that can be raised and lowered at will, allowing you to compensate in real time the changing weather situation.

Connecting Your Turbine to a Battery

The battery is ultimately where you will store your wind energy until you disperse it into your electronics. A good deep cycle battery stores power per amp hour and the depletion rate can be tracked along the speed that it actually recharges.

You should never completely take all the power out of your battery either. Because if you completely deplete a battery it will be extremely hard to recharge it, if it can be recharged at all, I learned this the hard way with some of my own early forays with deep cycle batteries.

Let me just tell you. It's not like your cell phone battery that you keep constantly propped up at 10%! To be on the safe side you should always keep your battery charged up to at least 50% of its capacity, otherwise the battery is going to go bad!

And since these kinds of batteries aren't exactly easy to come by, you are going to want to hang on to them as long as you can. There are two main types of deep cycle batteries that you can use for a micro wind turbine. They consist of flooded and sealed batteries.

As the name might imply, a flooded battery is a battery that has the power cell inside of it routinely flooded with electrolytes (battery juice for the uninitiated). As opposed to a sealed battery that keeps its electrolyte material firmly in place. Flooded batteries are generally cheaper and easier to come by than sealed batteries but they have the draw back of freeing up in cold weather.

Having that said, if you live in particularly cold environs you should always go for a sealed battery. The last thing you need is to wake up on a cold winter morning only to find your battery as frozen as the ice outside! Keep all f this in mind when you connect your turbine to your battery.

Understanding the Need for Inverters

For the most part, all of that wind energy we generate would be useless without a good inverter. You see, all power running from your turbine and into your battery works on a direct current (DC) whereas almost every electric appliance known to man runs on an alternating current (AC).

So in order to make life a whole lot easier on yourself you will need to run your direct current energy from your battery into your inverter so that it can be converted into an alternating current. The inverter is the conductor of your energy so be sure to have one on hand. You can usually acquire one of these for a reasonable price at your local hardware store.

Backup Generators

For the most part, you could effectively run a household on win power alone, but there is still a need for backup generators. These backup generators are useful for when the days are a little less windy, giving you that extra boost that you might very well need. A word to the wise however, if you are using kerosene, gasoline, or diesel generators, only use them outside, since the fumes of these generators can be hazardous to your health.

Chapter 3: Know the Rules of Your Community

If you are ready and able to construct your own micro wind turbine, the next thing that you should prepare yourself for is the reaction of your community. Are there any special rules and regulations in regard to having such projects?

If you are a home owner, one of the best ways to find out is to visit your local HOA (Home Owner's Association) they should be able to give you a clearer picture of just what is permissible and what is not. Otherwise you might want to go to your area zoning and regulations committee to get the scoop yourself. In this chapter we will discuss in further depths, just how you can know the rules of your community.

Building Permits

Unless you live on a deserted island somewhere you will probably eventually have to gain official permission to build through a building permit. This means inundating yourself with all of your local city ordinances, and state code protocols.

You need to contact local building authorities in order to get these things squared away.

And if browsing the internet doesn't find you what you are looking for, another good idea is to find a local building professional, and they should have the experience to lead you in the right direction.

Building permits aren't rocket science, they are just written legal permissions to build. These channels are open to anyone who requests them and are for just as much your own protection as well as your community at large. Make sure you make gaining a proper building permit a number one priority.

Electric Permit

People often get so caught up with what they are going to do to get their building permit that they often forget all about getting their electrical permit in order. Yep, that's right you may very well need an electrical permit in order to continue your work on a micro wind turbine.

Get yourself used to something called the "National Electrical Code" so that you can understand the legal mumbo jumbo of electric installation.

Or better yet consult a local electric professional who is no doubt familiar with the process, and let them help steer you along. An electric permit, just like a building permit is for your own safety, so make sure that you get one *before* you begin any electrical installation.

Conditional Use Permit

Just as it might sound, a conditional use permit is an additional permit given to ensure conditional use of a property for construction projects. If later on in the year for example, you foresee yourself adding on to the work that you initially constructed with your building permit, you may want to invest in a conditional use permit. These permits are meant t augment any exiting permits and permissions that you may already have.

Talk to Your Utilities

Even if you aren't connecting your turbine to the local power grid, you should still probably consult with the utility powers that be in your area. Admittedly, these guys have a monopoly on energy and you don't want to have one of them casting a suspicious eye on your own energy production.

And if you are planning on hooking your turbine up to the grid after all, its better sooner or later that you open up dialogue with the utility company directly.

There may be some release forms for you to fill out, and talking to them helps to streamline the process. By speaking to your utility company you can also learn how you can possibly sell excess energy you've produced right back to the electric company! Yes, its true, some utility companies will purchase energy that you produce, you just have to talk to them first!

Your number one contact at the utility company will most likely be someone referred to as a "designated manager" for renewable energy. These guys specialize in stuff like wind power and how it relates to the utility company, so they are definitely worth giving a try.

Network with Your Neighbors

More often than not, if we just tell our neighbors what we are up to in the first place, we will all be better off.

That way when you put up your tower you won't have your neighbors calling your HOA to say that you just installed a ballistic missile next door! Just communicate to your neighbors openly and clearly whenever you get the chance, and let them know what you are doing so their imaginations don't start running wild.

Networking with your neighbors could bring unknown benefits as well. Just think of your neighbors as potential colleagues and collaborators in the process. They may very well get excited by your idea, and you may even start a trend and inspire others on your block to follow suite. You never know, so network with your neighbors.

Chapter 4: Micro Wind Turbine Pros and Cons

Micro Wind Turbines, like everything else in this world, have both their positives and their negatives. There would be no point in glossing over the positive or negative aspect of the wind turbine, so in this chapter we are going to explore both. So let's take a nice long and sober look at all of the micro wind turbine pros and cons.

Inexpensive Installation

It doesn't cost that much to install your own micro wind turbine, this is true. The information presented in this guide has demonstrated this reality.

On a shoestring budget, with just basic supplies such as PVC pipe, tape, and a few other odds and ends you can have a really nice micro wind turbine without having to spend much money at all. The labor is free if you do it yourself and most of the parts you probably already have in the back of your garage somewhere, so all in all, you really can't beat it!

Save Money on Your Utility Bill

Saving money on those outrageous electric and heating bills can no doubt be a big motivator for most of us to set out in our wind turbine adventure. And according to the latest statistics, you could easily cut your electric bill in half after just one year's use of micro wind turbines. Half of your bill goes out the window from your first year of wind harvesting.

This is only the beginning however because if you keep at it, you can eventually reduce your bill down to zero. And it doesn't stop there, if you partner with your local utility company you can even send some of those energy savings back to them and generate real revenue of energy saving profits!

Many are shocked to learn that the utility companies pay top dollar for wind energy, but its true, even the grid based providers see an incredible money saving future with the power of wind energy.

You Can't Depend on the Wind

Ok, I hate to be a bummer here, but although we have so far sung the praises of micro wind turbines, there are some definite cons involved that you should be aware of. And one of the most glaring is the fact that you can't always depend on the wind to be there. Wind by its very nature is unpredictable.

This is a simple statement, and really it should seem like a no brainer, but yes, wind activity greatly ebbs and flows, and during some seasons you might find yourself in a veritable wind drought.

Wind itself can't be bottled up and stored in containers, the best you can do is bottle up your accumulated energy produced in a deep cycle battery. But really, this should be good enough.

Because even though wind does ebb and flow throughout the year and its intensity and durability depends on the area you live in, you can compensate for this by storing up additional batteries of energy when the wind is good. The wind itself is unpredictable, but if you plan ahead, you can mitigate the challenges that this fact presents.

Turbines Are Dangerous for Birds

Birds do occasionally get hurt from turbines. The turbine is a tall spinning structure, and sooner or later a bird will collide with them.

There is no way getting around this fact. But as bad as it might be to step outside and find a decapitated or otherwise disfigured bird, these incidents are few and far between. Recent studies have concluded that even the largest wind farms only kill a few birds on average.

It's not hundreds, its not even dozens, its just two or three birds a year who accidently wander into the blades. The death of any bird is said, but the figures show that it is extraordinarily rare.

And besides the rarity of actually collision, there are many things that can be done to minimize the potential for damage even further. Many new features on turbines offer up some great safeguards to help prevent the incidence of bird collision. As it stands right now, birds face much more grave danger from oil spills and extraction of coal than they could ever face from wind turbines.

Wind Power Helps the Economy

Back on the positive side of the spectrum, there I much of the way in good news when it comes to the things that wind can do for the general economy. The market for renewable resources such as wind power is helping to jumpstart economies all over the globe.

The revenue from the saved money that otherwise would have been spent on fossil fuels is tremendous. So leave those fossils in the ground where they belong and use wind power to grow the economy! When it comes to wind turbines a bit of magic *and money* is in the air!

Property Value Could Take a Hit

But although the general economy may be improved, there is some concern that personal property value could take a hit. There is truth in the fact that wind turbines can make your home lose value. They are considered a noisy eyesore in many communities, so don't be too surprised if your property value does go down if you place a micro wind turbine in your yard.

You might want t have a sit down discussion with your HOA, or at least a local realtor in order to figure out just what you might be up against. There could be no effect on your property value at all, but it's always much better to ask and find out, than to be surprised later on. So give your realtor a call!

Wind Turbines Promote Tech

Another great thing about wind turbines is the fact that it helps you to promote high technology. These turbines have many interchangeable features and when you link them up to inverters, generators and GPS systems, you will have yourself a very high tech device. For a device that utilizes something as basic and primal as the wind, it certainly does take advantage of and promotes a lot of great technology.

Conclusion: Just a Little Wind bit of Wind

It is truly amazing how something that we can't even see, the wind, could yield so much power. But ever since the first day that I became interested and involved with wind energy systems, I knew that I was on to something good.

To be able t utilize what mother nature provides for us for free, and then turn it into a net benefit for myself and family has been very satisfying. With just a little bit of wind I've managed to change my whole life. Now let's get out there and see what a little bit of wind power can do for you! Thank you for reading this guide!

Made in the USA
Las Vegas, NV
27 March 2022

46402478R00017